To

From

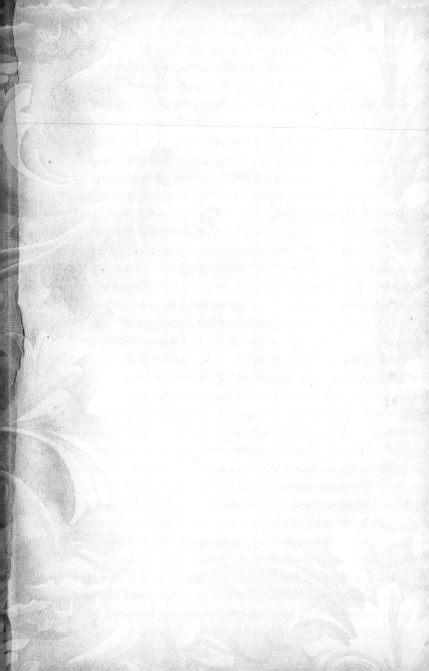

Celebrating the Joyful Season

A BETHLEHEM CHRISTMAS

CHARLES R. SWINDOLL

THOMAS NELSON
Since 1798

NASHVILLE   DALLAS   MEXICO CITY   RIO DE JANEIRO

A Bethlehem Christmas: *Celebrating the Joyful Season*
© 2007 Charles R. Swindoll, Inc.

Published in Nashville, Tennessee, by Thomas Nelson. Thomas Nelson is a registered trademark of Thomas Nelson, Inc.

Thomas Nelson, Inc., titles may be purchased in bulk for educational, business, fund-raising, or sales promotional use. For information, please e-mail SpecialMarkets@ThomasNelson.com.

Unless otherwise identified, Scripture quotations used in this book are from The New American Standard Bible® (NASB). © 1960, 1962, 1963, 1971, 1972, 1973, 1975, 1977, and 1995 by the Lockman Foundation, La Habra, California. All rights reserved. Used by permission. (www.Lockman.org)

Designed by LeftCoast Design, Portland Oregon.

ISBN 978-1-4041-0468-6
ISBN 978-1-4041-7498-6 (Custom Edition)

www.thomasnelson.com

Printed and bound in China

10 11 12 13 14 WA 5 4 3 2 1

*C*ontents

IN APPRECIATION

For years now I have wanted to re-visit the scenes in Bethlehem in a new and creative way. Because most of us are familiar with the nativity story, having heard it since we were children, it seemed to me that we needed to look at everything with fresh eyes. By approaching the familiar from a completely different perspective, I felt that much of the Christmas story would take on a deeper and far more significant meaning.

My hope was to tell the same old story, but this time as if I were the one personally involved in the events—first as Mary, then as Joseph, and finally, as the angel Gabriel.

As I embarked on this literary journey, I quickly realized I needed help! That help came from my son-in-law, Mark Gaither, who had already edited several of my previous books. In doing so, he had demonstrated creative skills in a number of ways. When I first mentioned my desire to write *A Bethlehem Christmas* in the first person, his eyes lit up like tiny torches! Immediately, Mark had suggestions to offer, which led to ideas that both of us became engaged in with growing enthusiasm.

In the weeks that followed, we enjoyed an ongoing dialogue as we probed various scriptural scenes, each one sparking an ever-widening circle of imagination. Not wanting these excursions to drift too far, we kept returning to the original New Testament accounts. With the additional assistance of careful research in historical volumes and extra-biblical sources we were able to add colorful details that help bring the ancient scenes to life in a relevant and reliable manner while staying within the lines of accuracy. Thank you, Mark, for the hours you invested in this creative project. I love your passion for excellence!

The result of our mutual effort is the book you are holding in your hands. Hopefully, these pages will open your eyes and feed your imagination in ways that make this story even more unforgettable.

I am also grateful to Terri Gibbs of Thomas Nelson Publishers. Thank you for your commitment to making this volume not just another book, but a work that will

endure. My hope is that it will cause many to
celebrate the sacred season and, at the same
time, realize what a treasure we have in the
One who makes it sacred.

Chuck Swindoll
Frisco, Texas

Your request has been granted! Elizabeth will bear you a son. A very special son.

THE WAY MADE STRAIGHT

The Holy Place, with all its gravity and mystery, grabbed Zacharias by the senses and held him captive for what seemed an eternity. He tilted his head back and breathed in the mingled aroma of bread, incense, cedar, and the burnt flesh of sinners' substitutes. Ministering in the Holy

Place was a rare opportunity in the life of an ordinary priest, so he consumed every detail with his eyes, fully intending to return there in his mind for years to come.

It was darker than he imagined. Cedar paneled walls disappeared into the darkness nearly a hundred feet overhead before meeting a ceiling he could barely make out. Finely crafted furniture adorned God's enormous antechamber, and the gold implements appeared to be as holy as their purpose. Seven lights of a large golden lampstand flickered on his left. On the right stood a table with twelve loaves of unleavened bread neatly arranged in two rows of six. A few steps ahead, the altar of incense. A flat, square, surface standing three feet high, and overlaid with pure gold. And within arm's length of the altar, a thick linen veil separated him from the potentially lethal presence of the Almighty.

This was the place where men met God.

His task wasn't complicated. Twice each day, a priest slipped behind the outer veil with a censor of coals from the altar in one hand and a measure of incense in the other. It should only take a few moments, but Zacharias wasn't about to rush anything.

He stepped forward, poured the coals onto the altar and then covered them with a finely ground powder of spices and frankincense. A few moments later, he could barely see the blue, purple, and scarlet cherubim woven into the veil that hung between him and the Most Holy Place. As the smoky perfume rose to the nostrils of God, a faint breeze brushed the back of the old priest's neck, and for a moment, he felt certain he wasn't alone.

"Zacharias."

The elderly priest clutched his robe and fell back, nearly cracking his head on the stone floor. A man, dressed in a simple, linen shroud stood to the right of the incense altar, no more than two feet from where he had been working.

"Do not be afraid, Zacharias."

Startled, terrified, dumbstruck. He turned his body to lay face down, put his head to the floor, pulled his knees under him, and stretched out his arms toward the angel's feet.

"Get up, Zacharias. I am only a servant, like you. I am here with an announcement."

The priest raised his trembling frame to face the messenger, but could not keep himself from covering his head with his hands. "What does the Lord want with His servant?"

"Elizabeth, your wife. She is barren, is she not?"

"We had hoped for a child. We prayed for a child, but to our shame, the Lord did not find us worthy." Sobs rose from deep within the

priest, from wounds he thought long since healed. "We have been faithful to the Law; we have kept the Lord's Word; but the Lord is right in all His ways. I am not without sin."

The angel moved toward him. "Sin has not kept Elizabeth's womb closed. Your request has been granted! Elizabeth will bear you a son. A very special son!"

As the fear drained from Zacharias, something else flooded into the hollow of his chest. Something he hadn't felt for a long, long time. He searched for the right word. Relief? No. More than relief. Hope? Yes. Relief, confidence, joy, all combined into one. It was hope. Hope!

The laughter of the angel pulled him from his trance only to find that he was standing erect with his arms hanging naturally by his sides. The urge to cower under his hands was gone. The burden that had rounded his

shoulders and squeezed his chest had
vanished. His heart beat freely for the first
time in years.

The angel's laughter embarrassed him a
little, but he couldn't help but laugh with
him.

"Your son will be very special. In fact,
the Lord has ordered that he is not to drink
wine or strong drink, he is not to eat or drink
anything from the vine; not grapes, not
raisins, not even the skin of a grape."

The priest's jaw went slack. "A Nazarite."

"Yes. A 'separated one.' For life. He will
be filled with the Holy Spirit even before he
is born."

"Why?"

"Do you remember the words of Malachi?
The very last words of Scripture? 'Behold,
I am going to send you Elijah the prophet
before the coming of the great and terrible

day of the Lord. He will restore the hearts of the fathers to their children and the hearts of the children to their fathers, so that I will not come and smite the land with a curse.' Your son is he, and you will name him Johanan, 'God's gift.'"

Zacharias felt his heart skip and his knees go weak. "The Forerunner! That means the Messiah is not far behind. No . . . this cannot be! No . . . no, my desperation has overtaken my senses. This is not real. *You* are not real. Oh, the devil is a crafty one to toy with my hopes. And to use my longing for a child and the Hope of Israel against me is just the kind of evil I would expect from him!"

The angel's smile dissolved and his countenance grew stern. The smoke of the incense stirred as he quickly moved toward Zacharias and took him by the shoulders. "Look at me. I am no devil. I am Gabriel and

I have come directly from the presence of the Lord to bring you this good news. And because you have listened to your own voice instead of the Lord's, you will remain silent until the forerunner of the Christ has a name."

Zacharias opened his mouth to repent of his faithlessness, but the words melted like wax and formed a ball in his throat. He was mute. And in an instant, he was alone.

"You have found favor with God."

Chapter 1

MARY

Most people in Nazareth farmed
for a living; my father was a
stone mason. We raised some
crops, but construction work within a day's
journey from home kept him busy, so he was
gone for much of the week. But he always
made it home by sundown for the Sabbath.

Each week, he would tell me which road
would bring him home. Then that Friday,

I would wait for him at the edge of town.
And for much of my childhood, this was our
own unspoken arrangement. Every week
I surprised him, and every week he acted
surprised and delighted to find me waiting.

He liked to sing while he walked, so the
lines of a favorite temple song usually crested
the ridge before his smiling face came into
view. For me, seeing him appear on the
horizon was like seeing the sun rise! And
even as I grew older, I never outgrew the urge
to dash up the road and throw my arms
around his neck.

On our walks back to the house, we
would talk or sing. Then, after washing
with water from the well, he would help us
prepare for the Sabbath meal. On the last day
of each week, without fail, we set aside the
cares of the world and entered the rest that
the Lord had commanded. We ate, and sang,

and told Father the village news. We listened
to him tell ancient stories about Abraham,
Moses, Joseph, and David. I especially
enjoyed hearing about Sarah, Ruth, Esther,
and Deborah. Father said I would have made
Deborah proud!

The memories I keep of those walks back
to the house, with just my Father and me,
and the Sabbath celebrations we enjoyed as
a family are more valuable to me than any
worldly possession. They are all that remain
of the simple times I enjoyed with my family.
And they are what helped heal the wounds
we suffered soon after.

Nazareth was a tiny village of no more
than 180 people—many of them relatives—
and it felt cut off from the rest of the world.
The town sat in a shallow basin high above the
Jezreel valley, far enough from the main roads
to be missed by anyone not looking for it—

and *no one* looked for it. Roman soldiers often stayed in Nazareth because it gave them a good view of the territory, so our regular contact with Gentiles made us undesirable to other Jews. We were often the subject of gossip and prejudice. Honestly, though, many in Nazareth earned us the bad reputation. Some of the families were too friendly with the soldiers and their daughters paid an awful price. Father told us to respect the men but to keep our distance.

A remote, tight-knit community like ours was both a blessing and a curse. We were one big family, so we took care of each other, but everybody knew everything about everyone. I loved most of the people, but I also longed to get away from them! So, when Father announced that it was time to consider my future—meaning marriage—I was horrified. Most of the young men I knew had been playmates—they were too much like brothers for me to think of any one of them as a potential husband. But I trusted my father.

Within a few weeks he introduced me to the man who would become my husband—Joseph, the son of Jacob. A carpenter like his father, both men traveled often with my Father. Joseph lived in Cana, a town not quite two hour's walk from Nazareth. From the moment I met him, I knew I would be happy. He was handsome and serious, with a shy smile that made me feel weak. It revealed the tender, humble strength that women long for and so rarely find in a man.

After meeting Joseph, I greeted *two* men on the outskirts of Nazareth each Friday because Joseph began to celebrate the Sabbath with our family on a regular basis. I could see in Father's eyes that he was pleased Joseph and I were bonding so quickly. But his joy was tinged with sadness, if only a little. He had done the duty of every good father. He had set the standard of manhood for his little girl—and then arranged for her heart to be stolen by another. And, I freely admit, I was falling hopelessly in love with the carpenter from Cana.

Within a few months, our parents had signed the marriage contract. This meant we were effectively husband and wife, though we were forbidden to live that way. The betrothal period is a torturous custom for which I see no good purpose—like setting food before a ravenous man and telling him not to eat until tomorrow. But we were obedient. Strictly. We didn't want anything to spoil our first night together.

We would have to wait twelve months for the marriage feast to take place. Twelve long months of loving and longing. But it was the happiest ache I had ever known.

Eight months later, both families were
making plans for the home-taking ceremony
and growing closer every day. One morning—
it was a Thursday—my mother, brothers, and
sister went to Cana. Father was working
somewhere, and I was tending to my chores
at home, glad to have the house to myself
for awhile. That's when it happened. The
conversation that would change everything.

I was hunched over a grinding wheel,
pulverizing grain into flour—something
I would normally have done in the courtyard
with the other women, but I wanted to be
alone with my thoughts. I was quietly humming
one of the hymns I learned from Father when
a gentle breeze suddenly blew through the
room. When I saw my shadow forming on the

floor, I instinctively turned to see what light could shine so brightly during the day. And just as my eye caught a glimpse of a warm, yellow light, a voice like none I had ever heard before broke through the silence.

"Good afternoon, Favored One! The Lord is with you."

The light came from a man dressed in white, a shining angelic presence that would have frightened me to death except his greeting confused me. First, that sort of greeting would have been reserved for a person of high station, not a lowly teenaged girl. Second, what did he mean by "The Lord is with you?" I thought, *Who am I to the Lord?*

After a brief pause, he continued. "Don't be afraid, Mary."

I was in such awe, I didn't think to be afraid.

"You have found favor with the Lord; you will become pregnant and bear a son, whom you will name Yeshua, 'the Lord saves.'"

Suddenly, I was overcome with fear. I had just gotten used to the idea of marriage and was looking forward to the wedding feast, but I had tried not to think about the pain and danger of childbearing. Still, I heard myself reply, "I will be honored to bear my husband a son. Hopefully, many sons!"

"No, Mary," the angel interrupted. "You will conceive before the wedding feast."

"How can this be? Joseph and I . . . no. I have not been with a man, ever. Nor will I, until my wedding night!"

The messenger stepped forward and gestured for me to be quiet.

"This will be no ordinary child. He will be called the Son of the Most High, and the Lord will give Him the throne of His ancestor,

King David. And He will be the king of Israel forever!"

As the angel spoke, I listened. I heard every word and still remember them to this day. The words seemed to pass through me, yet they were familiar. I recognized several phrases from the temple songs my father sang; especially, " . . . His kingdom will never end." I looked intently into the messenger's eyes and asked, "Messiah? Are you saying I will bear the Messiah? How will this be if I am to conceive *before* my wedding night? Certainly, the Lord would not have His Anointed One conceived in sin!"

The angel slowly nodded in agreement. "You're right. Joseph will not be the father, nor any other man. The Lord's Anointed will not be the seed of sinful people. The Holy Spirit will come upon you, the power of the Most High will overshadow you, just like the

cloud of His presence settled over the tent of
meeting in the days of Moses. That's why the
child will appropriately be called 'the Son of
God.'"

I could not imagine how anything like
this could be true. It sounded reasonable and
absurd at the same time. And the look on my
face must have revealed my uncertainty.

"Elizabeth, your relative was barren into
her old age and underwent the change.
Yet she is six months pregnant! So, you see,
nothing is too hard for the Lord."

My heart nearly leapt from my chest.
I knew of no woman more deserving of a
child than Elizabeth, and for this we had all
prayed earnestly. Just like Sarah's son, Isaac,
Elizabeth's child would be a miracle. I
determined I would not laugh in disbelief like
Sarah, but I needed a moment to think about
all the angel had said. As I pulled a stool

under me and sat down, the angel offered
a patient smile.

I sat for a moment, trying to understand
what the Lord had asked of me. Somehow
I realized that I had a choice to make. I could
refuse. But Father's words rang in my ears. He
had said at least a hundred times, "Mary, obey
first; understand later."

I dropped to my knees, bowed my head,
and whispered, "I am the Lord's to do with as
He pleases; let what you have announced be
done." And I began to sob uncontrollably.

I was relieved to be utterly surrendered
to the will of the Lord, but I was terribly
afraid.

The following morning, I faced the
obvious dilemma: how to tell my family.
Everyone except my father had returned

"Now in the sixth month the angel Gabriel was sent from God to a city in Galilee, called Nazareth, to a virgin engaged to a man whose name was Joseph, of the descendents of David; and the virgin's name was Mary."

(LUKE 1:26)

home by sundown, and I was able to avoid
having to explain why I was so pensive the
night before. My two brothers were too young
to notice much and certainly didn't care about
what goes on in a girl's mind. My little sister
was a handful, so she kept Mother
distracted most of the time. All night long,
I weighed the only two options I had. If
I waited until my belly bulged before telling
anyone, I would sound like a fool, and a
blasphemous one at that! The other choice
was to tell them right away, before any girl
could know she was pregnant. Then, at least
my family would see that the only way
I could have known about the baby was by
the word of the Lord.

I decided to wait until my father returned
home so I could tell my parents and Joseph
at the same time. And all day Friday, I could
barely suppress a smile. For as long as I could

remember, my father had told us stories from the Scriptures, and in some way or another, he managed to see the Lord's promise of a Messiah in each one. As each story came to mind, my hand unconsciously rested on my belly. Surely they would see the blessing as clearly as I did, but it would perhaps require more faith than they possessed.

That afternoon, I met my father and my husband-to-be on the ridge just outside of town and walked with them back to the house. They washed themselves and joined in the preparation for the Sabbath meal. After sundown, we ate and talked and laughed like always. Usually something we said or did during the meal would give Father an excuse to tell a story from the Scriptures. But I decided to take the initiative.

"Father, sing us the song Isaiah wrote."

My father looked baffled for a moment,

then asked, "Okay, which one? He wrote several."

"The 'Prince of Peace' song."

He sat up from his reclining position, put his hands, palms down, on the table, breathed in deeply, and bowed his head as if to gather his thoughts. Then he began to sing.

The people who walk in darkness
Will see a great light;
Those who live in a dark land,
The light will shine on them.

You shall multiply the nation,
You shall increase their gladness;
They will be glad in Your presence
As with the gladness of harvest,
As men rejoice when they divide the spoil.

For You shall break the yoke of their burden and
the staff on their shoulders,

> The rod of their oppressor, as at the battle
> of Midian.

For every boot of the booted warrior in the
battle tumult,

> And cloak rolled in blood, will be for
> burning, fuel for the fire.

For a child will be born to us, a son will be given
to us;

> And the government will rest on His
> shoulders;
> And His name will be called Wonderful
> Counselor, Mighty God, Eternal Father,
> Prince of Peace.

There will be no end to the increase of His
government or of peace,

> On the throne of David and over his
> kingdom,

To establish it and to uphold it with justice and righteousness
From then on and forevermore.
The zeal of the Lord of hosts will accomplish this.

When he finished singing, no one could speak. No one in the world loved the Lord more than my father, which made me love my father completely. As I looked around the table, I found Joseph staring at him with a look of admiration and love that gave me great peace. Their shared devotion to the Lord cemented their bond as men and made the world safe for me.

What I was about to say would put my trust in them to the test. And while I knew that my bond with my father and Joseph would be strained to the point of breaking, I knew the truth would eventually restore us.

After a few moments of silence, I spoke.

"I have wonderful news that will be difficult for all of you to believe."

Every eye around the table rested on me. When I had everyone's attention, I continued.

"The promise of that song is about to be fulfilled. I am carrying the promised Son; the Prince of Peace grows inside me as we speak."

As I looked around the table, my eyes met blank stares. Time seemed to stop for several minutes as everyone sat in stunned silence. Eventually, my father leaned forward and searched my eyes. "What did you say?"

"Two days ago, I was visited by a messenger from the Lord, an angel. He was sent to tell me that I would conceive a child by the Holy Spirit and would give birth to the Son of the Most High. It's just like the song, Father. This is how the Messiah will come to Israel. When the prophet told us about Immanuel, 'the

Lord with us,' what did he say?"

My father answered, shaking his head in confusion, "A virgin will be with child and bear a . . ." Suddenly, his eyes widened, and then became slits through which I saw an icy glare. He had never looked at me that way before. It broke my heart, but I understood. If what I had said were not true, I would have been guilty of blaspheming the Lord in the worst way.

When I finally looked at Joseph—my beloved, my betrothed husband—the anguish in his tear-filled eyes made me feel like I had plunged a knife into his heart. He rose slowly to his feet and stumbled out of the house into the darkness. It would be more than three months before I saw him again.

My mother leaned on my father's shoulder and quietly sobbed. She was a simple woman. Quiet. Sensitive. Selfless. Father stimulated my mind, but Mother's childlike purity taught me how to be uncritically, unconditionally devoted. She cared not whether what I said was true, only that it caused pain for the most important people in her life, including me.

Father put his arm around her waist, pulled her to her feet, and guided her to the door. They slept on the roof that night, as they often did when they wanted to be alone. That left me to tend my younger brothers and sister. After getting them settled for the night, I pulled my mat to the far side of the room and lay down.

As I drifted off to sleep, I cried. But not for me. I wept for the people I loved. As for me, I felt a peace no woman could ever know. Despite the pain and confusion and sorrow that covered our household, as well as the world beyond our little house, I had the truth. Hope grew within me—literally. I was headed for a very different future from what I had imagined, but I felt safe walking the path that lay before me. I had no idea how my little Yeshua would be "the Lord's salvation," but even before I could feel Him move, He had already begun to save me.

The next morning, Father decided I should stay with relatives in Judea rather than endure the shame of an unwed pregnancy in Nazareth. At first, my stubborn streak resisted, but when he mentioned Elizabeth's name, my heart rejoiced. I knew this was the Lord's doing, so I immediately agreed. Within a few hours, I was on the road to the city of Jezreel to join a caravan south. I was to travel with a family my father trusted, but he told me to keep the reason for my journey a secret.

I obeyed my father's instructions and

remained silent, although it broke my heart to possess such a wonderful truth and have no one to share it with. For countless generations, women had hoped to have this blessing, to be the mother of the Messiah. Then, to have received such grace, only to be treated like a daughter of dishonor, grieved me more than words could express. I resolved to walk with dignity and silently rest on the truth I shared with the Lord and no one else.

After three days of travel, I arrived in Hebron, where Elizabeth and Zacharias lived. I hadn't seen Elizabeth in a few years and knew she wasn't expecting me. But our families had been close and she always seemed to favor my company. While I was eager to see her, I worried how she would react to the reason for my coming.

As I entered the courtyard of their home and called Elizabeth's name, a squeal of delight came from the rear of the house, followed by the odd sight of a grandmotherly figure with a motherly bulge coming to greet me. She threw her arms around me and squeezed me tight as she exclaimed, "The Lord has blessed you more than any other woman, and blessed is the fruit of your womb! Tell me, why have I been blessed to receive a visit from the mother of my Lord?"

When I heard these words, the reservoir of strength I had struggled to maintain burst in a flood of tears. I was no longer alone. Someone understood. Somehow, Elizabeth knew my joy and shared my burden without my having said a word.

"How could you know? I haven't been with child for a week, and the news could not have come before me!"

Elizabeth replied, "The child I carry is the forerunner of the Messiah. So, as soon as your

voice reached my ears, my son leapt for joy!
You see? He already knows the Christ."

Another fit of sobs overtook me as
Elizabeth pulled my face to her shoulder
and held me tightly.

"Mary, you are to be commended for
believing the Lord's announcement with a
whole heart. Rest assured, my dear, not only
are you blessed, you *will be* blessed. Be
patient."

I don't know why Elizabeth's words
gave me such comfort and hope, but the
Lord knew what I needed and His sovereign
control perfectly met my need. At that
moment, something came over me and I
sang a song I had never heard before. The
words were mine but they weren't from me.

"My soul exalts the Lord,
And my spirit has rejoiced in God my Savior.

"For He has had regard for the humble state of
  His bondslave;
For behold, from this time on all generations will
  count me blessed.
"For the Mighty One has done great things for me;
And holy is His name.
And His mercy is upon generation after generation
Toward those who fear Him.
"He has done mighty deeds with His arm;
He has scattered those who were proud in the
  thoughts of their heart.
"He has brought down rulers from their thrones,
And has exalted those who were humble.
"He has filled the hungry with good things;
And sent away the rich empty-handed.
"He has given help to Israel His servant,
In remembrance of His mercy,
As He spoke to our fathers,
To Abraham and his descendants forever."

The Lord was gracious to give me Elizabeth. I can't imagine how difficult it would have been without her. And I was glad He had sent me to be with her during the last three months of her pregnancy.

The Lord is gracious to spare old women the difficulties of carrying a child. Her aged body needed lots of care, and I was overjoyed to make life easier for her. Zacharias, unable to hear or speak, retreated from public life and spent his time researching every detail about the Messiah he could find in the Scriptures. He had written an account of his angelic visit, but few believed him. When Elizabeth emerged from her seclusion soon after I arrived, opinions started to change. Her wiry gray hair, aged body, and protruding belly became the talk of the hill country, and people began to wonder where and when the Messiah might appear.

I thought I would remain in Hebron until she gave birth, and perhaps help her with the baby until she was back to full strength. But a message came from my father instructing me to return home.

Ever the protector and provider, he had arranged for me to travel with friends. I hated to leave my kindred heart in Judea, but I missed home, even if I had no one there to share my joy. I would again have to trust the Lord's timing and that He would prove faithful to my obedience. "Obey first; understand later."

The journey back to Nazareth was much more difficult than the trip up to Hebron. Neither my body nor my mind was my friend. I tired easily and worried how I would be received now that my belly was beginning to bulge. Even so, I made no effort to hide my condition.

I arrived home to find my family going about their normal business, which they dropped immediately when I entered the common courtyard near the house. My brothers wrapped their arms around my knees and buried their faces in the folds of my outer garments. My sister hung on my arm asking endless questions about my journey, while mother fought a losing battle with her tears. Her embrace felt especially good, and I was glad to be home.

After washing my feet at the well, my brothers pulled me into the house while my mother and sister laughed. After my belongings were put away, Mother said, "Your father arranged for the neighbors to fetch him when you arrived. He will probably get here tomorrow." Then she flashed a wry smile. "And if I know him, it'll be early."

She knew Father well. Early the next

morning, I awoke to find him playfully
shaking me and whispering for me to get
up. His smiling face was close to mine and,
for a moment, I felt like I had my father back.
But I dared not presume. When he had put
me on the caravan in Jezreel, he had been
the dejected father of a disgraced daughter.
I couldn't be sure who was greeting me that
morning.

"Mary, come with me. I have something
to show you."

I quickly threw on my outer garment and
followed Father across the courtyard to the
main road leading out of town. I could barely
keep up as we crested the ridge and started
down the slope toward Cana.

"Father? Where are we going?"

"It's better if you see for yourself,
daughter. I will tell you only this: the Lord is
gracious; more merciful than you can

imagine!" And with that, he began to sing.

Gracious is the Lord, and righteous;
Yes, our God is compassionate.
The Lord preserves the simple;
I was brought low, and He saved me.
Return to your rest, O my soul,
For the Lord has dealt bountifully
with you.

We sang that song again and again in
the time it took us to walk to Cana. When
we arrived at the home of Joseph's family
we found them hard at work, building a new
addition to the main house. As we approached
the property, my father shouted a greeting,
to which a voice called back. Just then,
Joseph popped up from behind a half-built
stone wall and immediately caught my eye.
He stood frozen for a moment, looking rather

dumbfounded with sweat dripping from his nose and stone dust falling from his hair. As we stared at one another, I couldn't ignore the pounding of my heart.

He dropped his tools, darted to me, and enveloped me in a crushing embrace. Then, suddenly aware of the little paunch between us, he quickly released his grip and backed away slightly, darting his eyes between my face and my tummy as if to ask, *Did I kill him? Is he okay?*

"He's fine! He will live!" I laughed.

Joseph sighed heavily and led me to a seat in the little courtyard that was formed by the main house and the adjoining rooms his brothers had built when they were married.

"I've missed you," he said. "In fact, I thought I had lost you forever! When you announced that you were pregnant, I thought you had . . . I thought you and . . ."

"I know," I said, not wanting to hear him actually say the words.

"I went up to Jerusalem to pray and seek the advice of an expert in the Law. For weeks I wept, and prayed, and tried to determine what I should do. And just when I came to a decision, something or someone would change my mind. Then, once I was able to overcome the pain enough to think clearly, I sought the Lord's council. Then, I met the most remarkable man."

"A priest?" I asked.

"No. He was just an old man. Another worshiper. But the wisdom he had!"

Joseph's eyes filled with tears as he shook his head. "The teachers of the Law were all in agreement. For the sake of my family's reputation, for the sake of my own dignity, to honor the Lord, and even to preserve our nation, they said it was my duty to have you

stoned for your sin. But the old man . . . well, I kept praying, asking for the Lord's direction. Finally, I decided that it would be best for me to have the marriage contract voided through divorce.

"But then something wonderful happened. I had been in the temple for several weeks, listening to various teachers, wrestling with my anguish, and praying to the point of exhaustion. I fell asleep in a remote cloister and, sometime during the night, a man—an angel—came to me in a dream and told me that everything you had said at the Sabbath dinner that night was true."

Joseph paused for a moment, then put his hand on my belly.

"Mary, you are the mother of the Messiah! The angel said we are to name him, Yeshua, because he will save his people from their sins!"

"We?" I asked. "The people of Cana and Nazareth will not likely receive a visit from an angel. You and I know the truth, but almost everyone else thinks I carry your child or, worse, the child of some nameless Gentile soldier. Did the angel say that you must take me as your wife?"

"No."

"Did he say that you *should* take me as your wife?"

"No. He merely answered the one question that haunted me day and night: Had you played the harlot?"

"So, the angel didn't compel you. This blessing is *my* burden. I cannot escape the scorn that will certainly follow me, but you . . . this hardship doesn't have to be yours. You have a choice."

"No, I don't have a choice. To divorce you would be to embrace a lie. Beside the matter of integrity and the honor of caring for the Lord's Anointed . . . I love you, Mary. I don't want to live without you."

The relief I felt cannot be described. Joseph's words were even more healing than those of Elizabeth. And the joy that flooded me washed away any resentment or bitterness I might have had—for anyone. My husband-to-be and I were united in our obedience to the Lord and shared a seamless intimacy. We were bound together by our vows, by our love, and by a sacred, secret truth.

In three weeks, our wedding feast would declare our legal union to the world, but our physical union would have to wait.

Our wedding feast was a small affair. Neither of our families were wealthy and given the circumstances, only our relatives and close friends wanted to attend. After the celebration, we moved into the new, one-room addition to Joseph's family home and lived as husband and wife, with one exception. Joseph continued to sleep on his mat in the main house. I agreed with his suggestion that we refrain from marital relations until after the child was born. He thought it fitting that I give birth to the Christ in the same state in which He was conceived. And he wanted this decision to be our public witness to the fact that this pregnancy was special.

The whispering among the neighbors continued, as we expected, but we had the

confidence of our families. Most of them, my
father included, accepted our story, although it
seemed to us that they understood it as the
official version of events, not necessarily the
truth. It was an uneasy truce. If we didn't
talk about it, they weren't obligated to take
a definite stand for us or against us. As far as
they were concerned, if Joseph was content,
they had no reason not to be.

After a few months, the time for me
to deliver drew close and everything was
falling nicely into place. That is, until the
government ordered a census and each
family was required to travel to the husband's
ancestral city. Joseph's family descended from
David, as did mine, which meant we would
have to register in Bethlehem of Judea.
Because we couldn't leave the homestead
unattended, the families in our clan would
have to take turns making the five-day

journey southward. My expected delivery
date was still a month or more away, so we
felt sure we had plenty of time to make the
trip, register, and then return home.

The early Fall weather cooperated and
a borrowed donkey carried our provisions,
but the journey was more difficult than either
of us had expected. My feet swelled when
I walked and my whole body ached when
I rode, so Joseph insisted that we stop to rest
often, usually against my protests. Most nights,
Jewish families along the route provided lodging,
but with so many people traveling for the
census, we were occasionally forced to sleep
outside under the stars.

It was one of the longest journeys I had
taken since I was a little girl. Seeing the
distressed, hopeless looks in the eyes of the
other travelers troubled me, and it explained
why my father chose the seclusion of

Nazareth to rear a family. Even with the
presence of Roman soldiers, we avoided
exposure to the evil that had taken up
residence in Jerusalem and had slowly
consumed the hope of Israel. The closer we
got to the holy city, the more intensely I felt
the darkness that had poisoned its heart.
Joseph noticed it too, but simpy said he
wasn't surprised.

By the time we reached Bethlehem, nearly
a week after we had started, I was exhausted.
The trip had taken a heavy toll on me. I had
begun to feel unusually warm and couldn't
go very far without a privacy break. To make
matters worse, the tiny town was burgeoning
with people—something we hadn't
considered. Joseph searched the town for
a household that wasn't already filled with
pilgrims, but none could be found. Inns were
notoriously filthy and innkeepers infamously

shifty, yet these, too, were unable to accommodate more people. We briefly considered traveling farther south to stay with Elizabeth and Zacharias, but I couldn't bear the thought of two more days of travel over the rough mountain terrain.

Our only remaining option came to us by way of a kind family who agreed to put their animals out to pasture so we could use their stable. As harsh as that sounds, it actually turned out to be very cozy. Where the pathway leading to town curved around one of Bethlehem's many steep slopes, someone had carved a large room out of the hillside. Joseph dutifully cleared the ground and scrubbed the walls and low-hanging ceiling to remove the smell of animals. It was a crude shelter, but it kept us out of the elements and a low fire warmed the chilly night air.

Once we were settled, I rested while Joseph and several thousand other men worked their way through an entangled and corrupt registration process. After several days, he was nowhere near finished. I, on the other hand, was getting close to delivering the baby. By our reckoning, it was early. The delivery should have been no less than three weeks away. As Father used to say, "While the Lord's timing is perfect, it's rarely convenient!"

As I dozed one afternoon, a dull ache gripped my waist and squeezed the breath out of me. I called for Joseph and ran to the pathway in a panic, but he would be gone for hours. I had attended many childbirths, so I calmed myself and began to arrange our little shelter in preparation for the baby. A spare tunic would be his swaddling. I made a little bed in the feeding trough with fresh straw and one of Joseph's old outer garments. I even managed to draw some water from a nearby well before the pains made moving around too difficult. I didn't feel much like eating but forced myself to eat some dried dates and raisins to keep up my strength.

As I lay there in my little, secluded birth room, the sun drifted lower and finally out of sight to my left. I hadn't noticed the billowy clouds hovering over the Judean wilderness until they glowed a brilliant orange. Bethel, "the house of the Lord," lay in that direction. Somewhere between there and where I laid, the travail of childbirth had taken the life of Rachel, who named her child, "son of my sorrow." Jacob changed it to Benjamin, "son of my right hand." Suddenly I feared that giving Israel a savior might come at the cost of my own life.

To calm my nerves, I tried to remember one of the temple songs Father sang so often.

Marshal your troops, O city of troops,

for a siege is laid against us.

They will strike Israel's ruler

on the cheek with a rod.

"But you Bethlehem Ephrathah,

though you are small among the clans

    of Judah,

out of you will come for me

one who will be ruler over Israel,

whose origins are from of old,

from ancient times."

Therefore Israel will be abandoned

until the time when she who is in labor

    gives birth

and the rest of his brothers return

to join the Israelites.

He will stand and shepherd his flock

in the strength of the Lord,

in the majesty of the name of the Lord his God.

And they will live securely, for then
his greatness
will reach to the ends of the earth.
And he will be their peace.

When I thought of the sorrow that overshadowed Judea, when I recalled the hopeless look in the eyes of the families shuffling around Israel to pay tribute to Rome, a warm, contented feeling filled me. My little son of peace would change all of that. And suddenly I didn't care what happened to me.

As evening fell, the pains intensified and came more rapidly. Joseph returned to find me moaning through a wave of pain and rushed to my side. He tried to make me more

comfortable and gave me some water, then ran back into Bethlehem to find a midwife. After a few more waves of pain, he returned with an old woman, who immediately took charge. She arranged her supplies, asked a few questions, and then chased the men away, leaving just the two of us and her little granddaughter to help.

There are no pains like those of childbirth. None so intense. None so hopeful. Only the words of the midwife reminding me that I would soon be holding my baby kept me focused on the reason for my anguish. Why such great joy must always come out of such deep sorrow, I don't know. But the moment the baby comes, all distress vanishes.

It was well into the night when the old woman laid the helpless Hope of Israel across my tummy and wiped Him clean. For a little less than nine months, I had talked to Him, sung to Him, felt His every move, and looked forward to this very day when I could finally touch His skin. Someday in the future, He would be the Shepherd of Judah, the Mighty One of Israel, but as I stared at the wriggling, cooing life that came from my body, He was simply my son.

The midwife expertly tore Joseph's tunic into wide strips, wrapped the baby tightly into a little bundle, and laid Him beside me. Once she finished tending to me, she sent the little girl to bring the men. Joseph entered first, looking worried and relieved at the same time. I reassured him with a smile and held the baby out for him to see. He was followed by a group of other men and their families, all of whom had heard about the events in town and had come bearing gifts. As the friendly people of Bethlehem celebrated with us—the men laughing and slapping poor Joseph on

the back, the women trilling and fussing over
how handsome our baby was—I could look
at nothing else.

Later, as the baby slept peacefully on the
little bed I had made in the feeding trough,
our visitors continued to enjoy our good
fortune. But their conversation came to an
abrupt end when a band of shepherds
approached from the wilderness. The eyes of
the oldest one roamed the stable, searching
intently for something. And when they landed
on the trough, he broke his stride and crept
forward with a look of awe on his face. Our
visitors nervously retreated, allowing the five
men a clear path to the stable as Joseph
stepped toward the lead shepherd and said,
"Good evening, men. What brings you in
from the fields?"

Without breaking his gaze, the shepherd
said, "The child. He's in a feeding trough."

Joseph offered an embarrassed chuckle. "Yes, we've had to make do. We're here for . . ."

"He's . . . He's in a feeding trough," the shepherd said again as he turned to the others and smiled broadly. When he turned back to Joseph, he apologized for the intrusion and began to explain the reason for his amazement.

"We were in the fields on the far side of that ridge when a man dressed in white clothing appeared before us. He nearly frightened us to death because he made no noise and Nathan here has ears like a Sand Cat. He greeted us and said he had a wonderful message . . . intended for us!"

He looked around at the others and laughed.

"No one even talks to us, much less sends a messenger! So we were suspicious. But he insisted. He said, 'I bring you this message of great joy and it's intended for everyone in the world. In Bethlehem, the city of David, there has been born a Savior, who is the Messiah, the Lord! And this will be how you will find Him: He will be carefully wrapped, lying in a feeding trough.' At that point, we thought his mind had been lost in the desert, but then . . ." The shepherd looked sheepishly at the astonished men and women nearby, and then at his companions. With a little encouragement, he continued.

"Then, the sky broke open and the desert became as day. An army of shining men flew from the clouds, some blowing trumpets, and many more shouting, 'Glory to God in the highest, and on earth, peace among all people with whom He is pleased!' This went on for the longest time, and we couldn't help but join the praise. It was the most astonishing sight imaginable, and if I hadn't seen it with my own eyes, I don't know that I would have

believed it. Then, the multitude turned and flew toward the clouds, followed by the first messenger.

"When they were gone, we immediately came to Bethlehem to see the child. And here He is. Just like we were told."

The other visitors marveled over what they had heard. Some ran back into town to tell others.

"The child . . . He's the . . ."

"The Messiah?" Joseph offered. "Yes."

"No. More than that. The angel called Him 'Lord.' This child is the Son of the Most High—God in human flesh! And He's not here for Israel only. He's here for the whole world."

I found the words of the shepherd to be sobering. I had come to accept that the child I carried was the long-awaited Messiah, but was He the Savior Israel was expecting?

My father, as well as all the faithful men in my family, believed that He would be our king, that He would rise to power, take the throne away from the evil men who now occupied it, cleanse the temple of corruption, drive the Romans from the Promised Land, usher in a new era of security and prosperity, and ultimately conquer the whole world. But did they expect that He would be the Almighty Creator in human flesh?

It occurred to me—call it intuition— that perhaps we did not fully grasp the full meaning of "Son of God," and that the Lord's plan was far greater than any of us could imagine. Immediately, the words of the angel in Joseph's dream came to mind: "Name Him, Yeshua, because He will save his people from their sins." What, exactly, did that mean?

It was far more than I could grasp that night in Bethlehem. Somehow, in the weakness

of a baby born in a lowly stable, the power
of the Almighty had come to earth. It was
a mystery that would occupy my mind on
many nights as I nursed God's Son and kissed
His tiny face.

"How I loved her!"

Chapter 2

JOSEPH

I had never met anyone like Mary before. There were lots of girls of marriageable age from good families in Cana and the surrounding towns, so when my father first mentioned a potential match for me in Nazareth, I chaffed at the idea.

"Nazareth!" I laughed. "You would choose a consort of Roman soldiers for me to marry?"

"Set your bigotry aside for a moment, Son.

Not all Nazarenes have been polluted by Gentiles. She's from a good family."

"Then why do they choose to live within spitting distance of a Roman garrison?" I snarled.

Father smiled patiently and paused for a moment. "They have lived there for many generations, as have many of the clans descended from David. They've been there since our people's return from exile. So, tell me, why should they let a pack of dogs chase them away? Besides, the father of the girl likes the seclusion. Eli says he would rather rear his family in the company of Gentiles than the compromising Jews who live here along the trade routes. And I'm inclined to agree."

Father always had a gentle way of explaining things so that if you were wrong about something, you knew it without feeling belittled. He knew my temperament. My desire for Hebrew purity—something I got from him—used to make me unnecessarily harsh. I realized that I had judged and condemned the girl before knowing anything about her.

"I'm sorry, Father. I should have known you would make a careful choice for me. What's her name?"

"Mariam."

"Hmmm. 'Beautiful.' Is she?"

"That's not for an old man to judge. And besides, you only wish her name meant 'beautiful;' it means 'rebellious.'"

"Is she?"

"For our sakes, let's hope so."

A week later, my father and mother took me to Nazareth to meet Mary and her family, and to dine with them. We approached the house and greeted her father, who invited us to wash at the well before sitting down for the meal. His three youngest children gleefully splashed water over our dusty feet, thoroughly soaking my outer garment. And as I rung out the water, Mary emerged from the house with her mother. Upon seeing her, I scrambled to my feet and Eli began the introduction.

I can't, to this day, recall what he said. Every other sight and sound faded away as I studied the woman who would become my wife and the mother of my children. Mary was beautiful, but not in the way a Greek would judge beauty. She was older than I expected, with strong, angular features and dark skin from working in the sun. What made her most attractive—to me, at least, but apparently not the majority of men—was the look of determined wisdom I saw in her eyes. She looked directly into mine, obviously

searching them for clues to my character.
I respected that and found her uncommon
strength to be exciting.

After that first Sabbath meal together,
I visited her regularly, always within sight and
sound of her parents. Each week, I learned
more about the remarkable woman Eli and
his wife had nurtured. As my love for Mary
grew, so did my respect for Eli, whose
knowledge of Scripture would have qualified
him to be a scribe. And in some respects
he was. The care that he took shaping and
polishing stones was surpassed only by the
diligent crafting of his children. Even the
youngest could recite enough hymns to put
a priest to shame. (That is, if a priest in that
day could feel shame.) Moreover, his little
ones delighted to learn about the One their
father loved and served.

After a very few weeks, I knew that Mary was a woman I could make a life with. I told my father that no one could have chosen a more perfect woman for me, and that I would like for him to arrange our pairing with her father. I could tell he was pleased and relieved to hear it. A marriage is a uniting of two families, not just a couple, so he and Mother had a vested interest in our happiness.

After a brief negotiation between the two fathers, our families and close friends gathered at the Synagogue to witness our betrothal ceremony, where we exchanged vows and heard the reading of the marriage agreement. The silver ring I slipped upon her finger declared to the world that we were married— husband and wife. However, it would be a full year before the home-taking ceremony. Only the barbaric societies that surrounded us would cause a woman to be sold like chattel and be removed to a strange household the same night. I would follow the traditions of our fathers and take no less than twelve months to win Mary's heart. Our love would need to grow strong before blossoming in the marriage chamber and bearing the fruit of future generations.

As the months passed and I grew closer to Mary's family, I was amazed by how similar Eli was to Father. They were not nearly the same man in temperament; my father was an incorrigible tease with a cynical sense of humor. Eli laughed only when it made sense to laugh and had almost no grasp of sarcasm. But both men saw everything in the world in relation to the Lord's promised Messiah. For them, all of human history—every event— was preparation for His coming. And given the events of the last few generations, no one could fault them for their eager anticipation.

This became especially clear to me when our families gathered in Eli's home to celebrate the first night of Hanukkah, the "Festival of Rededication." Upon lighting the *shamash* lamp and the first lamp of the festival, the patriarch began the story of victory in a somber, dramatic tone—clearly pitching his delivery to the children.

"We celebrate Hanukkah because the Lord honored the courage of righteous men with a miracle."

The children hushed and leaned forward.

"Judah then—as now—was not free. Gentile interlopers dominated our people and sought to pollute their faith with the worship of false gods. When some refused to play the harlot with other gods, the Seleucid dogs

slaughtered our mighty men, robbed the temple, and set up their own altar. Then they threatened to kill any Jew who did not sacrifice in accordance with the king's command.

"But one man, in the city of Modein, a priest named Mattathias would not compromise, even when the sword was put to his throat. When one of his neighbors stepped forward to play the harlot and sacrifice to another god, the priest put his hand to the sword and killed him. Then he killed the general who ordered the sacrifice. Then he led all of Judah in a revolt against the enemy of the Lord.

"Later, when the courageous priest was about to die, he called his sons around him and said, 'My children, live passionately for the Law and give your lives for the Covenant.

Do not fear what sinners will say, for their success will come to ruin. My children, be courageous and grow strong in the Law, for by it you will gain honor.'

"Then his son, Judah the Hammer, took up his sword and defeated the Gentiles and gained independence for Israel. And when they entered the temple to restore the sacrifices, and to light the lampstand, all of the sacred oil had been defiled except for one container—enough for one day. But in faith, they lit the lamp as the Lord had commanded . . . and it burned for eight days! Enough time for the priests to prepare more oil for the temple!"

And, with that, the children threw their arms in air and cheered. The adults around the table encouraged them by adding their own shouts of joy.

As the celebration died down, he continued. "But . . ."

The children responded by looking concerned.

"When Judah the Hammer died in battle, his brother, Jonathan, led the nation. But he was not like his father, Mattathias."

At that point, Eli drifted. What he said next was not for the children. I can't even be sure it was for us. But with a faraway look, he lamented the servitude of Israel.

"He compromised with the enemy and asked the Romans for protection. And had himself declared High Priest . . . by Gentiles."

Eli turned his face to the ceiling. Great tears rolled down the sides of his anguished face as he sobbed, "Made High Priest by Gentiles! . . . not by the Lord, but by Gentile kings! And now, Caesar's puppets and petty criminals rule the sanctuary of the Almighty and dress their crimes in priestly robes. How long, O Lord, before You send Your Anointed One—the Messiah—to break the bondage of sin and deliver us?"

By now, my father had buried his face in his hands and the women had turned from the table to cry. Mary gathered the children in her arms and gently rocked as they hid their little faces in her garments.

As the two families quietly mourned the corruption of the temple, the flame of the first lamp continued its merry dance—just as it did one hundred sixty-two years earlier. The people of Judah had rejected spiritual compromise and cleansed the temple of corruption, and against all probability, a faithful little light refused to go out.

Somehow, I knew in my heart that Israel's hope was not far away.

I once heard a rabbi say that hope burns brightest during the darkest of nights. On one particular Friday, the sun set on my life and I endured what I now call "my dark Sabbath."

As had become my custom, I accompanied Eli home to conclude the week in keeping with the Lord's commandment. As the sun set and we reclined at table for a particularly sumptuous meal, Eli laid a cloth over the bread, handed me the cup of wine, and asked me to recite the sanctification. It was a particular honor for me. I knew that this was his way of telling me that the spiritual care of his daughter was in my hands. I had recited the sanctification many times in my own home, but on this occasion, I treated it with special care. And as we said the last "amen,"

I returned Eli's gaze to let him know that I would care for his daughter at any cost, even my own life.

Much of the meal is a blur in my memory. I usually took the initiative in telling stories about our week at work or entertaining everyone with funny anecdotes about my family. The women sometimes scolded me for encouraging rude behavior in the boys. But on that evening, I was too distracted by a sudden appreciation for how much I had come to treasure Mary. This was more than the initial attraction I had for her, and more than the strong desire a man has for a woman. That night, as I sat across the table and caressed her with my gaze, I deliberately set aside a safe place in my heart and sanctified it just for her. It would be her place. A place of refuge where she could come and hide

from the world. A place were she was free to be what no other person would allow. A place to be afraid, hopeful, joyous, angry, or even unreasonable. It would be her Sabbath rest whenever she needed it. It was hers without reservation, condition, or cost. And I looked forward to the day when she would find it waiting, trust that it would always be there, and enter it to stay. How I loved her!

The laughter and singing usually gave way to more serious discussion on its own, but that evening, Mary requested a song from her father, a song about the Messiah. As he sang of the wonderful king, a sickly knot formed in the pit of my stomach as I watched Mary's tension mount. This was leading somewhere, and my instincts told me it wasn't going to be good. I had to make myself breathe during the long silence that followed Eli's last note.

Then, after describing a most unusual story,
Mary informed us that she was pregnant.

The words hit my chest like a boulder.
I sat stunned as she continued with a
preposterous, blasphemous story about
conceiving the Messiah and the invisible
Creator behaving in a manner that seemed
to me like the deviant gods of Rome. A wave
of questions flooded my mind. *Who was the*
father? Was she taken advantage of, or did she
consent? How could I have been so wrong about
someone I knew so well? Is she insane? Is she in
love with him? Does she not love me? Why would
she do this?

I looked across the table at Mary to find
her gazing at me with obvious compassion,
which outraged me. Was her delusion so
complete as to believe what she said? Or,
worse, her deceit so profound as to feign

concern for the lives she destroyed? The room began to spin and I felt my stomach rebel. I had to get outside.

I nearly tore the door off its hinges, ran into the night, and didn't stop until I stood on the ridge outside Nazareth. Exhausted, I sank to my knees then sat for hours in the darkness, staring across the plain and into the night sky. When I was a child, I had found comfort in the vast expanse of stars, a symbol of the Lord's power, permanence, and unchangeable character. So, I found the appearance of a new light—a bright dot high above the horizon —a little unsettling. But my anguish would allow no other thoughts for very long before the utter absurdity of my circumstances overtook me. Each time I recovered, a new dimension of this tragedy invaded my mind and brought with it another spasm of sobs.

As the horizon turned light blue and then pink, I made my way home. My parents, though grieved and bewildered by the turn of events, advised me to delay making any decision regarding Mary. It was wise advice. One moment I wanted to rush to her side, the next I wanted to wash my hands of her. But one constant remained through all of my pain and confusion: an unrelenting love for Mary.

My father had instilled in me a love for the Law. We memorized it, meditated on it, and applied it to every aspect of our lives. The Law was the birthright of every son of the Covenant, and it was by the Law that we communed with the Lord. But that Law demanded that an adulteress be taken to the place of execution and stoned to death.

Mary's announcement brought the two great loves of my life into mortal conflict. To love one, necessarily meant the death of the other.

The dilemma was agonizing. I felt I had become the plaything of a cruel, capricious universe that delighted to put earnest men in no-win situations for its own amusement. But Father encouraged me to think another way. He said, "In all my years, I have never known the Lord to be cruel. A dilemma for which there is no answer is an invitation to learn something new from Him. In situations like these, seek Him. Wait. Make no decision until He gives you clarity."

My father explained to Eli our intention to do nothing immediately, for which he was grateful. In the meantime, I decided to seek wisdom through fasting and prayer at the temple in Jerusalem. While most of the priests

could not be trusted, many teachers of the
Law met there. And I hoped the solitude
would help me learn what the Lord seemed
determined to teach.

The temple complex was, by far, the most
impressive sight in Jerusalem. The towering
structure presided over vast courtyards and
porticos, surrounded by high, gleaming white
walls. The temple was the centerpiece of
Hebrew Law, the Lord's provision for those
who found themselves at odds with His holy
commands, those who needed restoration.
Other nations had their thrones; we had an
altar—a blood-stained means of grace where
sinners, by faith, found forgiveness.

Each morning by sunrise, I entered the
Golden Gate, passed through the Women's

Court to the Court of Israel for the morning prayer service, the first of three offerings each day. After the morning offering, I usually joined a cluster of men for individual prayer and begged the Lord's wisdom until the afternoon offering. Then I listened to the rabbis teach in the courtyard until the evening offering, after which the temple usually emptied; that is, except for pathetic, lost souls like me, who roamed the temple precincts looking for something invisible and intangible—something we couldn't describe and only hoped existed. For without it, we would remain eternally anchored in our pain and confusion.

This went on for weeks as I fasted, prayed, broke fast, ritually washed, sacrificed, worshiped, and sat under the teaching of rabbis of every conceivable influence. Then, after one particular evening offering,

I retreated to a remote part of the temple
to pass another night in solitude. I arrived
at my customary spot to find an elderly man,
neither praying nor sleeping, but idly waiting.

"I'm sorry," I said. "I didn't expect to find
someone here. I'll find another place."
Then I turned to leave.

"Please. Don't go. I'm actually here for
you."

"Me?"

"Yes. I'm here every week, but today I'm
here for you. People tell me that you have
barely set foot outside these gates for many
weeks. How long?"

"Eleven Sabbaths."

"Eleven! I didn't realize it was that long.
Tell me, what would keep a young man
hidden from life for so long?"

I hesitated. Other than asking questions

of the teachers, I had kept silent about my reason for being in Jerusalem. But he was the first to ask, so I decided to hazard a response.

"I'm waiting for . . . well, I suppose you would call it an answer."

The old man laughed and asked, "What question could take three months to answer?!"

I resented his laughter and, as I opened my mouth to respond, a wad of angry words caught in my throat. The old man was quick to notice and put a reassuring hand on my shoulder. When I had regained my composure, I said, "It's not so much a question as it is a solution to a dilemma. I came here to learn more. And I have. But the learning hasn't brought me any closer to an answer. It has only made me understand how much more complex the problem is than I realized."

The man pulled me toward the outer wall to sit, and as night enveloped the temple, I told him my story. He followed each detail and asked questions. His responses validated my thoughts and assured me that I was not unreasonable. Then I shared with him everything I had learned under the rabbis, the Scripture I had studied, the insights I had gained.

At the end of my long discourse, we sat in silence for a few moments. Finally, I asked, "What are your thoughts?"

A look of recognition crossed his face and he expressed my dilemma perfectly. "You are caught, young man, between two of the Lord's greatest attributes. His justice and His mercy."

The tightness in my chest released just a little, which allowed me to draw in a long, refreshing breath. Someone understood the

problem better than I, and for the first time in months, I felt hopeful.

"Yes," I said, "I have come to see the Law as my friend, not my enemy. Because we have the Law, Israel is not like the godless nations who live in the fear of kings, who grow and wither like grass and whose laws do the same. We know right from wrong. The penalties for sins are consistent and reflect their seriousness, and those who honor the Law enjoy lives that are free of sin's consequences. To pursue justice honors the Lord."

"But?" The old man raised his eyebrows and leaned forward.

"But . . . He also loves mercy. Hosea the prophet was instructed by the Lord to ignore the Law's demand that he stone his unfaithful wife. As a priest, he was to maintain a strictly pure household, yet the Lord instructed him to buy his harlot-wife off the slave block and return her to his home. Despite her sin, the Lord restored her former place of honor in the priest's household, as his wife!

"But I am not a prophet. the Lord has not instructed me to disregard the Law. The Law demands that I honor Him by carrying out justice . . . which means I must execute the one I love. The experts in the Law all agree. In fact, they say it's my duty to every family in Judea and Galilee to stone her. Yet mercy demands that I honor the Lord by setting aside the required penalty under the Law and let her live.

"How can I reconcile justice and mercy?"

By the old man's smile, I could tell he had an answer.

"Tradition tells us that where we now sit is the very place where Abraham faced that dilemma. How confusing it must have been for him to hear the Lord's command to lay his only son on an altar and sacrifice his life. Obedience seemed to have been the enemy of mercy.

"How do you reconcile justice and mercy? Why, there's no need to reconcile friends! With the Lord, they are never enemies. They only appear so because we cannot see what He sees.

"Do you remember what Abraham did?"

It was a question a child could answer. "He obeyed the Lord's command," I replied matter-of-factly.

The old man leaned forward and put a hand on my arm. "Did Isaac die?"

"No."

He squeezed my arm and shook it as he said, "Think! Why?"

The significance of the story began to dawn on me. I looked over the man's shoulder to see a column of smoke rising from the alter, illumined by the moonlight. "Because the Lord provided a substitute," I said.

"Yes! But notice that he first had to obey. Abraham didn't allow the clash of justice and mercy to hinder his obedience. He trusted the Lord's character without first having to understand it. Then, *after* he obeyed by faith, the Lord revealed to Father Abraham what he could not see. His responsibility was to obey and allow the Most High to administer justice and mercy. And always remember, we are Abraham's seed . . . because we obey."

"So, you're saying that to obey, I must stone the love of my life?"

"No. This issue of obedience—and the reason you and I are here—is of far greater importance to you than you realize. Greater than you. Greater than what to do about Mary. Besides, these so-called experts have not instructed you well. You have not been asked to stone anyone."

"But I thought the Law demanded that . . ."

"Was your betrothed wife caught in the act?"

"No."

"Are there any witnesses or someone claiming to be the father?"

"No."

"Then how do you know she's guilty of adultery?"

"Because I'm not the father!"

"Have you not also considered another possibility? . . . Perhaps she's telling the truth."

"But her story is so . . . outlandish. It's insane!"

"Unless it's true. And you don't know. You may divorce her, but you cannot convict her. If you are to be righteous, you may cancel the marriage contract; no one expects you to wed a suspected adulteress. But expect no compensation, and do it quietly so as not to humiliate her or her family."

The old man gave me a lot to think about. After a few moments, he pulled himself up by the column with a grunt, patted me on the head, and left the temple. I tucked my coat under my head, curled up, and slept peacefully for the first night in months. I had found the invisible, intangible something that allowed my life to move forward. I determined to do what was right and proper as the Law demanded, but to pursue it with mercy.

Sometime during the night, I dreamed that I was standing outside Mary's home and

saw her open the door from the inside. When she stepped out, I could see that she was nearing the time to deliver her child. Just then, an angel appeared beside her and said, "Joseph, son of David, do not be afraid to take Mary as your wife. She has told you the truth. The child she carries was conceived by the Holy Spirit and she will give birth to a son. You are to name Him Yeshua, for He will save His people from their sins."

When the angel disappeared, Mary noticed me and smiled as if she expected me to be standing there.

The walk from Jerusalem to Cana took almost no time. I didn't stop to eat or sleep along the way. When I arrived home, I barely greeted my parents before telling them that the wedding feast must take place soon and we should break ground on the new addition to the house right away.

"Hold on, wait a minute," my father said, as he held me by the shoulders and guided me to the courtyard to sit with Mother. "What happened? We sent you to Jerusalem to let you release your burden and heal your heart. You were to determine the best way to handle the divorce and decide whether to press charges in the courts. Bringing an adulterous woman, pregnant with some stranger's baby, into our home as your wife was not, and is not, an option!"

By the end, he was nearly yelling, but Mother put a hand on his arm, which always helped him calm down.

I waited for a moment and then said, "My time in the temple taught me so much.

Not at first, but later. And I had determined to divorce her discreetly and not press the adultery charges."

"Very sensible," my father said as he turned to Mother. "Better than she deserves."

"But . . . an angel came to me in a dream . . ."

"Ugh . . ." Father rubbed his forehead as if kneading pain out of it.

"And he told me that Mary was telling the truth. The child she carries is the Messiah and He was conceived of the Holy Spirit. He is no ordinary baby; He's the Son of the Most High!"

Mother gasped as Father quickly stood up and faced the other direction. I had never seen him rub his forehead harder.

After a few moments, he turned to face me. Obviously working hard to contain his outrage, he said, "Look, your love for Mary is touching. And if you had told me that you wanted to bring her home despite her sin, I would have admired your forgiving spirit, and might have overlooked your clouded judgment. But, your devotion has you imagining things. For three months, you barely ate or slept. I know. I had friends checking on you and sending me updates. Your imagination has given you permission to pursue this folly."

"No," I said sharply. "First, a wise man taught me the role of faith in obedience. Then a messenger of the Lord told me the truth about Mary."

"Okay," Father reasoned, "let's just suppose Mary carries the Messiah. Have you considered the life you are accepting? People will think you couldn't wait for the home-taking before taking Mary. Or they will think you have no problem wedding a woman made filthy by another man's sin. You'll lose respect. Shame will follow you wherever you go. You aren't guilty and you aren't a fool. You deserve a better life than this!"

"If, indeed, Mary is telling the truth," I reasoned back, "and I put her away, then I have embraced a lie, have I not?"

Ordinarily, my father loved debate. Only this time, the issues were more than hypothetical. His silence told me he wasn't so sure about his position.

"In fact," I continued, "divorcing her would be my public declaration that the Son of the Most High is illegitimate."

He sat in silence with his eyes closed, drumming his fingers on his head.

"Father, I know that what I have been asked to do will complicate my life. No one

wanted the simple pleasures of working and
rearing a family more than I. But I must obey.
And how wonderful it is that obedience
should restore the love of my life to me!"

My father didn't speak to me for two
nights and days. I knew that he was sorting
through everything I had said and simply
needed time and silence to think. Finally, he
reluctantly gave his blessing. We would prepare
for the feast and complete the additional
room for the home-taking. When I suggested
going to Mary's house together to break the
news to the family, Father informed me that
she was gone; she had fled somewhere south
to have the baby in private, perhaps never to
return. But having anticipated my reaction, he
had already sent word to Mary's father, asking
him to beg her to return.

The next morning, the two of us began building the new addition.

Long ago, the leprosy of Rome had infected Jerusalem and begun to spread north into Galilee. The love of money was consuming the flesh of Israel. Rich Jews loaned their poorer brothers money to pay taxes to Caesar, charging exorbitant interest. Caesar, in turn, helped the wealthy evict those who couldn't repay their loans. Slowly, but surely, the sons of the Covenant were being taxed out of the Promised Land.

Most of us lived far enough away from the big cities to escape the notice of the tax collectors, but the power lust of Augustus continued to spread. Shortly after Mary came to live with my family, Caesar's worldwide tax decree reached Cana and we were compelled to register. Every male of a given tribe would have to stand before a Roman Censitore to declare under oath his lineage, the name of his wife and children, the lands and other assets he owned, including cattle, buildings, clothing, and jewelry. Sometimes this included an assessment of the man's character to determine if he was moral by Roman standards. This was eventually dropped in Judea and Galilee, but not before countless Jews refused to be judged by any standard other than the Law of the Lord. And anyone who didn't register was subject to severe punishment, which always led to homelessness and poverty. Compromising Jews who cooperated with Rome gained land and wealth, while obedient Jews suffered for their faith.

As a descendent of David, whose clan originated in Bethlehem, I had to journey several days south to register along with my kinsmen. It would be a sad and unusual family reunion with men I had never met. But because Jewish blood runs thick, I found myself looking forward to seeing my extended family for the first time.

Mary was several weeks away from delivering the child she carried, so we felt sure we had plenty of time to make the trip. The registration process would go smoother with her there, and we dared not wait, so we set out for the Judean hill country with our provisions on a pack animal. We would travel south to a main road, head east across the Jordan, follow the river until we were clear of Samaria, then travel west across the Jordan into Judea. No self-respecting Jew would want to defile his feet with Samaritan soil.

I had made this journey many times
before, but now I saw everything through
new eyes. We were traveling not to honor the
Lord with a sacrifice or to celebrate a festival,
but to give an accounting of our lives to
Augustus, who considered everything we
owned his property. I felt unclean. Like
I was admitting that the Most High was
not my God, but a man. And the closer we
came to Jerusalem, the more this darkness
threatened to smother my hope. I also noticed
that the light in the eyes of the host families
near the holy city had grown dim.

It stood to reason. It was a dark time.
The throne of Israel sat empty, waiting for
the rightful owner—a son of Jacob—to
ascend it and to rule the world. But a usurper
had claimed the Messiah's seat through

intrigue and bloodlust. Herod—a descendant of Esau—was a cruel king who claimed the title "King of the Jews" and declared himself our supreme religious leader. To prove it, he built the most magnificent temple in the world in Jerusalem. But he also built the city of Caesarea around a temple in honor of Augustus.

I expected the journey to take five days, but Mary's condition was more delicate than either of us had realized. We rested often and lingered at each stop until I saw Mary's strength return. After long and tedious miles, we finally reached the little village of Bethlehem. I was discouraged to see it overrun with hundreds of families from all over Israel, Egypt, Syria, even as far away as Asia. Many slept beside the roads and in dark alleys. We would normally have hoped for the

hospitality of a local household, but every home was filled beyond capacity.

Zacharias and Elizabeth, Mary's relatives, lived another two day's journey south over rugged terrain, but Mary was too exhausted to travel on. I became worried. She looked pale and lacked the exuberance I was accustomed to seeing. As a last resort, I considered the public lodging just outside the village. These were filthy establishments run by shifty characters, and most often used by caravans along the trade route. But even these had become miniature cities.

I had nearly lost hope when a young man caught my arm and spun me to face him. I recognized him from one of the families we had approached earlier.

"My mother could not get you out of her mind. She sent me to find you. We have a stable on the north side of town and we can put the animals out to pasture. You can stay there. Follow me. I'll show you."

He led me back toward the village and then followed a small road down the north face of the hill to a wide, manmade niche in the rock with a low ceiling. For generations, livestock sought refuge from the elements, and the stench from the ground and limestone walls bore witness to the fact. I had only two choices. Make this place habitable for Mary, or sleep in the fields and risk injury by weather, wild animals, or robbers. I opted for the safety of the stable.

After several hours of scraping and shoveling the ground, I put down a thick layer of fresh soil mixed with lime dust and covered it with clean straw. Then I washed the walls down with lye to cut the odor. By

the time I brought Mary to the stable, we
were hungry and weary from travel, so almost
anywhere would have felt welcome. She tilted
her head up, looked deeply into my eyes,
kissed me, and with an approving smile, said,
"What a cozy place you have found for us.
And we don't have to share it with anyone!"

Although she acted like it was a palace,
I couldn't get past the fact that my wife had
to sleep in a stable.

If the tax registration process were an
honest exercise, it would have taken no more
than a day to complete. But the Censitore and
his team of suspicious Censuales could smell
impatience. Anyone too eager to conclude
business and return home would suddenly
find the process very complicated or the

tax rate usually high without a stiff bribe.
A fair rate was a waiting game that required
standing in lines and completing meaningless
legal tasks. And for me, it took several days.

After a particularly long day of negotiation,
I returned to the stable to find Mary doubled
over with delivery pains—much earlier than
we expected. Once I was sure she was settled
and secure, I found a midwife who agreed
to help us. I brought her the supplies she
requested and then obeyed her command to
leave them in privacy. I retreated to a clearing
beside the road leading to town as it curved
around the hill. To keep warm, I built a fire.

As I waited, memories of the past few
months occupied my mind. I marveled at the
wisdom of the old man in the temple. After
I had obeyed, the Lord revealed what I could
not see. I recalled the bitter tears of Eli and

his oddly worded plea: "How long, O Lord, before You send Your Anointed One—the Messiah—to break the bondage of sin and free us?" I also struggled with how to make friends of the apparent enemies, Justice and Mercy. How can the Lord take His own Law seriously if He pardons transgressions without penalty? And how can He pardon transgressions without denigrating His Law? And I puzzled over how Abraham's experience on the summit now occupied by the temple related to all of this.

Most of all, I wondered how the child in Mary's womb might hold the key to understanding everything. For centuries, the sons of Abraham had looked forward to the birth and rise of the Messiah, but how many expected that He would be the Son of the Most High?

I still had difficulty understanding what that meant. All I really knew was that I had to apply the lesson I learned from the old man: "Obey. The Lord will provide."

News spread quickly in Bethlehem and, before long, my little camp fire had become a bonfire, thanks to a small army of townsfolk. The women huddled near the blaze as the men stood in small groups and complained about the tightening grip of Rome on Judah's independence. The conversations going on around me became a distant murmur as I stared up into a cloudless sky at the vast expanse of stars. And my eye quickly settled on the new light I had noticed in Nazareth several months earlier. As I wondered about its significance, a single name repeatedly rose above the murmur. Augustus. Augustus. Augustus. Augustus.

In Latin, "Augustus" meant exalted one.
Early in his reign, he claimed that the
appearance of a new light traveling across the
sky was the spirit of Julius Caesar entering
heaven as a god. And as Caesar's heir, he
claimed to be the son of a god. I couldn't
suppress a chuckle as I thought of the
many ironies—sad as they were. Those who
worshiped the one true God served at the
whim of superstitious, unwashed pagans who
worshiped dead men. In Jerusalem, a son of
Esau sat on the Son of Jacob's throne, building
monuments to the Most High and to Jupiter
with money minted from the blood of faithful
Jews. Somewhere in Rome a man exalted
himself as the supreme ruler of all mankind,
while the King of all Creation would, this
night, enter the world in a stable.

I suddenly felt alone in the world, yet

strangely connected to the Lord. He had made me the sole caretaker of the world's most wonderful secret, and I wondered if anyone else noticed the new light twinkling in the sky, high above the horizon.

Within moments, the midwife's little assistant excitedly summoned me to the stable. As Mary came into view, my eyes met hers and then settled on the tiny wonder she held in her arms. My little Exalted One. My Light. My King. My Deliverer. My Messiah. My Yeshua. My Savior.

*God's promises
always exceed
expectations.*

Chapter 3

GABRIEL

I know more than any mortal could, for I stand in the very presence of God and announce His decrees to people on earth. Yet, despite the timeless, heavenly perspective I enjoy as one of His heavenly messengers, one particular mystery is beyond my ability to understand: God's persistent, unrelenting love for people. It began before time and it will never end.

My specific role was to carry announcements concerning the Messiah, which I first revealed to God's servant Daniel. He lived more than five hundred years before the Messiah was to be born, during the reign of Belshazzar of Babylon. I had to do battle and overcome the forces of evil to reach the prophet, and when I arrived, I interpreted the visions he had received. I described the political events that would signal the coming of the Messiah along with a detailed timetable so that no one could overlook his arrival.

As instructed, Daniel kept his prophecy from the general public at the time, but recorded every detail in a scroll for future generations. He also shared his revelation with the king's astrologers and magicians, even going so far as to calculate the future position of the constellations when the

Messiah was to be born. Long after he was dead, long after the people of Judah had returned from exile, he anticipated and predicted the skies would signal the arrival of the King of the Jews.

World events unfolded exactly as they had been revealed to Daniel. The Babylonians gave way to the Persians, who were, in turn, conquered by the Greeks. Then the Romans became the rulers of Judea. The decree of Artaxerxes to rebuild the wall of Jerusalem established the time in which the people of Israel could expect to receive their king. And as the heavenly clock wound down, I thought, *Certainly, after all that I had announced—the signs, the times, the most explicit details recorded by Daniel—certainly, the people of Judah would be watching and waiting. Certainly, they would have no trouble recognizing their need for a savior. Certainly, they would*

anticipate and celebrate the arrival of their deliverer. Everything had been revealed. All the people of Israel had to do was watch the calendar, travel to Bethlehem as the prophet Micah later announced, and welcome Him.

But I am not omniscient. I could not see the future as God does. As the time approached, His covenant people didn't appear ready, which confused me greatly. But, as always, He had a plan. Knowing that Israel would be distracted or disinterested, He promised a forerunner through His prophet Malachi. As the time for the Messiah ripened, He sent me on a mission. I was now to announce the birth of the forerunner of the Christ to a priest in Jerusalem.

When I appeared to Zacharias, the father of the boy, I was excited beyond words. The plan announced more than five hundred years earlier was about to commence! I told the old man that he and his aging wife would give birth to John, the forerunner before the Christ, and that he would serve God in the spirit and power of Elijah. But, to my utter dismay, he resisted my message. He failed to believe me!

Did every Jew think that Israel was like an aged woman, too old to bear new life? Did they not understand that *God can do anything?!*

While I looked with sorrow on Zacharias for his failing hope, I admit that I bristled at his lack of faith. And by God's instruction, I struck him deaf and mute for the duration of Elizabeth's pregnancy. He would be a living symbol of Israel's failure. As a priestly nation to the world, it was their duty to proclaim God's Word and become an example of belief.

I returned to the throne room of heaven entirely dejected and confided in a fellow angel, "I know God's plans never fail, but

I fear this plan will not go as smoothly as I had anticipated." The next phase worried me even more.

God explained that the Messiah must be born of a virgin.

"Why a virgin?" I asked.

"Because He is to be My Son," He replied.

This took me by surprise, and I began to see that His plan involved far more than delivering Israel from the oppression of Rome, more than giving them political power and economic prosperity, more than merely fulfilling the promise of land to Abraham. I should have known the character of God better, having served Him as long as I had. His promises *always* exceed expectations.

He continued, "I announced My plan soon after the fall of Adam and Eve in the Garden. But don't fault yourself for failing to notice. Even Moses, who recorded My words, did not realize their full meaning. If you recall, I pronounced a series of curses as a consequence of disobedience. I cursed the woman to suffer anguish during childbirth. I cursed the man to toil for his sustenance. I cursed their intimacy to endure strife. I cursed the ground to produce weeds and thorns along with crops. But do you remember the first curse I pronounced?"

"Yes," I replied. "You cursed the serpent who deceived them to crawl upon the ground, and that, one day, the heel of her seed would crush his head."

The Lord God nodded in approval. "Yes, but you omitted a part."

"Do you mean where You said the serpent would bruise the heel of her seed?"

"Indeed, I promised that the offspring of the woman would destroy evil forever, but not without great personal cost. You see, My plan

has always been to save humankind from the affliction of evil."

"But, Lord," I asked, "can You not rid the world of evil simply by destroying Satan and all his angels?"

"No. Unfortunately, when the first man chose to disobey, he became infected with the disease of evil. And he passed it on to the next generation, and they to the next, so that all of humankind is inseparably bound to evil. To destroy all evil, I would have to destroy the people I have made, the people I love so very, very much."

As I thought about the problem of sin and evil, I realized the difficulty. Transgression of God's Laws—decrees that reflect His very character—must carry a penalty or they are meaningless. To forgive the sin without penalty would require God to deny His very character. Yet to eradicate sin would destroy the sinner.

Unable to resolve the dilemma, I asked, "How will You destroy sin and preserve the people?"

The Lord God glowed with pleasure at the opportunity to reveal the next detail of His plan. "I will provide a substitute—someone to pay the penalty of sin on their behalf."

"But who?" I protested. "How can someone pay for the sins of another if he dies paying for his own?"

"A very astute question," He answered. "The substitute must not have *any* sin of his own."

I was even more perplexed. "But Lord, the substitute would have to be a human in order to represent humanity, yet all of humanity has been infected with evil. Furthermore, this substitute would have to be superhuman in order to pay the penalty for all people, to die a death that would cover not just one sinner's penalty, but that of the whole multitude! What substitute can possibly suffice?"

After a short silence, God said, "God."

I stood dumbfounded. It didn't seem possible. And if it were, it didn't seem fair. Indeed, it wasn't! This was grace. So characteristic of Him, yet utterly beyond my ability to comprehend.

He continued, "I will send My eternal Son to be the Messiah. He will be the substitute. The Messiah will not be the son of a sinful, earthly father, but My Son, born of a virgin to preserve His sinlessness. The Messiah will be man. The Messiah will be God. Being the God-man, He will represent humankind, yet He will have no sin. Furthermore, after He dies on behalf of all humankind, He will conquer death by rising from the grave."

I could not speak. The perfection of His plan—so ingenious, so simple, so intricate—

left me even more amazed than seeing Him create the universe with a mere word.

"Do you see now?" He asked. "The first curse I pronounced in the Garden—the curse in which the woman's offspring would suffer the sting of evil—was a curse upon the Almighty. The Father will suffer the loss of His Son, who will suffer an excruciating death, matched only by His abandonment to suffering by the Spirit."

At this, I wept. The immense love of God was more than I could fathom. The selfless grace of God was beyond my comprehension. And for what? Creatures who neither desired Him nor sought Him, who not only failed to believe but who refused to believe. This will always remain a mystery to me.

As I considered how He would implement His plan, how the the Messiah would be born of a virgin, I noted that it would bring incredible

hardship on the chosen couple. It would call for unqualified obedience, complete submission. I humbly asked, "Can any such people be found in all of Judea or Galilee?"

"Yes," He said. "In fact, that is your next task. You are to go to a devout young woman, a virgin, who is betrothed to a spiritually sensitive young man. I have prepared them since childhood for this. They have been reared by godly parents and are therefore faithful students of My Word who earnestly desire to obey. The young woman is Mary. Go to her now. Tell her that she will be the mother of the Messiah."

"What about the young man?" I asked.

"Not now. I have much to teach him first. I will use this ordeal to prepare Joseph for the difficult task of rearing the Son of God."

I pitied the man for what he was about to endure. "Is there no easier way?" I asked.

"You already know the answer to that. Don't worry. I have a man waiting for him in Jerusalem. When Joseph's heart is soft, when he is ready to hear and accept My will, My servant Simeon will be there to guide him. Then he will be able to receive the announcement from you. Now, go."

I delighted to tell the young woman. Naturally, she was confused at first, but she never hesitated to obey. And while she fully understood the hardship it would bring, she saw it as the most wonderful honor any woman could receive. Her attitude and obedience qualified her for angelic service. But it was better that she was created for this purpose.

To help Mary endure the loneliness of misunderstanding until Joseph was ready, the Lord arranged for her to visit Elizabeth, whose heart He had prepared. In the meantime, I waited for the Lord's signal before appearing to Joseph in a dream. I knew he would be the greater challenge. It was a particular relief to me when I could assure him that Mary had not betrayed his love. And he, like Mary, never hesitated to obey the Lord God, despite the lifetime of difficulties it was sure to bring.

As the time approached for Mary to deliver the Christ, heaven could barely contain the excitement, so I was distressed by the response of people on earth. Elizabeth's unusual pregnancy and Zacharias's experience in the temple caused a sensation in the Judean hill country, yet very few anticipated the Messiah. The teachers of Scripture in the temple had certainly seen the prophecies of Isaiah, Daniel, Micah, and Malachi, yet no one truly sought the Christ. Bad enough that he would be delivered in a stable and cradled in a feeding trough, but the King of all creation was about to be born, and no one knew.

This was a mystery that would lead me to learn another lesson about God's plan. And it began with my next mission. I was to lead a contingent of several thousand angels to announce the Savior's birth to—of all people —shepherds.

The only class of people considered lower than shepherds were thieves. Even Gentiles were afforded more respect. Again, I found myself baffled by God's logic. Were the plan mine, I would have roused the sleeping world by trumpeting the birth of the Messiah in the temple and in the royal courts. I would have engaged the important people in welcoming the new King to earth. I would have caused a supernatural, dazzling, cosmic display to coincide with His birth so everyone would know that God had come from the heavens to earth in the form of human flesh.

But not God. He said, "I will announce

the birth of the Savior only to those who care to know it, only to those looking for a savior. Those who want a king to lead them into battle or a leader to make them rich will not know what to do with My Anointed One.

If the rich and the learned and the powerful care to find Him, they will have no trouble. I have made the time and place of His birth known to all mankind for many centuries."

So I found a small band of shepherds tending sheep in the fields within an hour's walk of Bethlehem. Once the Savior was born, I approached them quietly so as not to startle them too much, and then once I had their attention, I split the veil between Earth and heaven to reveal a host of angels praising God. And those Bedouins responded exactly as I had hoped. They leapt to their feet and joined the praise of heaven, then immediately set out to find the Christ in Bethlehem.

As the Lord God carried out His plan,
I began to see an important truth. Not every
heart is prepared to receive a savior, or to
recognize Him when He arrives. And this
saddened me. In heaven, our entire existence
revolves around the adoration of God and
every activity is a response to His perfect
will. I cannot imagine living any other way.
Humans pursue happiness and fulfillment
apart from Him. Some even think that
communion with God will mean the end of
personal satisfaction. Most are barely aware
that sin has separated them from the source
of their contentment and continue to live in
vain pursuit of cheap substitutes.

I suppose nothing has changed very much
since Adam's tragic choice so long ago.

I was briefly encouraged by the response
of the shepherds, but I soon fell into a deep
despondency. God noticed the sorrow on my

face and asked me to share my heart with Him.

"I don't understand, Lord," I sobbed. "The greatest event in all of human history has just taken place, an act of grace too wonderful for words, yet almost no one cared to notice. You know all things. You can see what I cannot. Please, tell me, is there any hope for humankind? You have sent the Savior. Will any receive Him?"

I felt the compassion of God envelope me as He answered. "Gabriel, My faithful champion, your concern for humanity reflects My own. Come, let Me show you something that will surely warm your heart as it does Mine. Look there in the temple. Do you see someone familiar?"

"Simeon. The old man you sent to instruct Joseph."

"He's there almost every day. I made him

a promise years ago that he would not die before laying eyes on the Messiah. There are many more just like him all over the world, though not all of them know it yet. They long to see the Savior and they faithfully go to their respective temples looking for Him. Soon they will see Him. Soon they will hear."

"Will all of them respond like Simeon? Will they receive the Savior?" I asked with eagerness.

"No. Not nearly as many as you would wish. But many will. Multitudes, in fact. And not only in Judea and Galilee. Look."

He directed my attention to a spot on the eastern side of the Arabian desert. There, a cloister of Magi preserved the traditions of the Babylonian and Persian astrologers. As they looked into the western sky, high above the horizon, a new light triggered a memory. One of magicians dug out

an old manuscript and rediscovered Daniel's calculations. And after comparing his charts to the sky, he searched the Hebrew Scriptures for the significance of Daniel's map of the stars.

He soon found his answer. A king! But not just any king. The King of the Jews. A King who would eventually rule the world.

The Magi knew that a delegation must be sent to investigate, so they elected a number of representatives and assembled an expedition to Jerusalem. (Where else would they expect to find a king than in the capital city?) They traveled more than three months to see the new King, and when they found Him, they did something extraordinary. They fell down on their faces and worshiped!

Unfortunately, not everyone responded to the news of Christ so favorably. The Magi inadvertently stirred Herod's jealously, which led to a hunt for the Christ child, not to worship Him but to destroy Him. His ruthless search led to the mass murder of male infants throughout the region, but the Lord God sent me to warn Joseph. I instructed him to take his little family to Egypt for safety, where they would live for no less than three years. Then I was there to summon him home to Galilee after Herod had died. But just to be on the safe side, Joseph elected to settle in Nazareth instead of Cana. In the seclusion of the little forgotten town, he would ply his trade, teach Yeshua all that he knew about the Law, the Prophets, and the Writings, and look for the day when he could explain that He was adopted.

As the boy grew in wisdom, stature, and in favor with God and men, I saw the drama that played out in Bethlehem repeated again and again. Most ignored Him, many rejected

Him, some recognized the Savior and, like the Magi, fell down and worshiped.

In time, I came to understand the grand truth behind God's plan. Those who want a Savior will find Him. And if they see Him as He is, they will worship.

My great hope for the sake of humanity is that wise men will continue to seek Him.